Original title:
Between Boughs and Ballads

Copyright © 2025 Creative Arts Management OÜ
All rights reserved.

Author: Elias Marchant
ISBN HARDBACK: 978-1-80567-455-9
ISBN PAPERBACK: 978-1-80567-754-3

Whimsy in the Whispering Thickets

The trees giggle, leaves in dance,
Squirrels debate, in a nutty trance.
A rabbit hops with a jaunty jig,
While frogs croon tales of a grand old fig.

The wind whispers secrets, just for fun,
As raccoons plot mischief, 'til day is done.
With blossoms that chuckle and tickle the air,
Nature's a jester, a funny affair.

Rhapsody of Blossoms and Breezes

Blossoms prance in the sunlight's wink,
Dandelions giggle, not caring to sink.
Breezy choirs sing, a funny refrain,
While butterflies chase a rogue, lively train.

Petals throw parties, their colors ablaze,
Confetti of pollen in sunlit displays.
Nature's a party, come join in the cheer,
With laughter so loud, you can almost hear!

Cadence of the Timeless Trail

On the trail of giggles, where shadows play,
An old turtle tells tales, in a cheeky way.
Where squirrels wear hats and act quite absurd,
And birds tweet jokes that are utterly blurred.

A rabbit with glasses reads stories aloud,
While a wise old owl giggles, oh so proud.
Nature's a comedy, a wild, funny show,
Come lose yourself here, let laughter flow!

Verses Woven in Nature's Tapestry

In threads of laughter, the wildflowers weave,
A tapestry bright that makes you believe.
A deer with a bowtie struts with finesse,
While hedgehogs play poker, no need to impress.

The sun beams a grin, the moon joins the jest,
As critters compete for the ultimate quest.
In nature's grand theater, the humor's intact,
With every new joke, joy's simply unpacked!

Poetic Roots and Fluid Branches

In the garden, worms wear ties,
Debating why the sun should rise.
A butterfly called for the vote,
While ants set sail in a tiny boat.

Trees gossip with their leafy friends,
Sharing secrets that never end.
A squirrel juggles acorns for fun,
While raindrops tap dance, just begun.

Cadences of the Calm

Birds rehearse their morning songs,
While frogs croak out their rights and wrongs.
The bees are buzzing, quite the sight,
Arguing who gets the best flight.

A cat naps on a sunny stone,
Dreaming of fish and a soft purr tone.
The breeze chuckles, whispers of cheer,
As clouds attempt to hold back a tear.

Eulogies for the Evaporating Day

As twilight tiptoes on the grass,
Even shadows seem to laugh, alas!
The sun waves goodbye, a playful flare,
While stars come out, just to compare.

Crickets claim the night, a warm embrace,
Lighthearted tales in a starry race.
And moonbeams spill like laughter's light,
Chasing dreams that take delight.

Fables from the Flora

A rose told tales of love so grand,
While daisies danced in a flower band.
Violets joked about their blue hues,
And lily pads put on stylish shoes.

The oak shared wisdom, deep and wide,
But the willow just swayed with pride.
Petunias giggled with their bright flair,
Swaying to tunes that floated in air.

Lyrics from the Leafy Lounges

In the park where squirrels dance,
Their acorn hats in odd romance.
The birds sing tunes of silly lore,
While shadows play on grassy floor.

The leaves exchange a snickered jab,
As rabbits wear a specious lab.
With little boots, they hop and prance,
As if they're in a comical dance.

Oh, the roses blush, they can't believe,
The antics of the dogs that cleave.
They chase their tails, with utmost glee,
While onlookers laugh beneath the tree.

So grab your hats and join the fun,
In leafy lounges, the joy's begun.
With every giggle, every grin,
A world of laughter we create within.

Poetic Reflections in the Sylvan Halls

In sylvan halls, the owls do cheer,
Wearing glasses, sipping on beer.
They hoot some rhymes, quite out of tune,
While critters dance beneath the moon.

The trees lean in to catch a rhyme,
With raccoon poets, oh, so prime.
Each joke a leaf that dips and sways,
In nature's laughter, bright array.

The moonlight glints on beetle's heads,
As they tell tales of monster beds.
With fluttering wings, they all concur,
What fun it is to be a blur.

So waltz with whimsy, frolic free,
In sylvan halls, join the jubilee.
Each whispered line, a playful shout,
In the woods where laughter's never out.

Songs Carved by Wind and Time

The breeze composes silly rhymes,
Of cats in hats and robins' crimes.
A gust brings forth an ancient tale,
Of snail races amid the gale.

The rocks giggle in their stone embrace,
As trees recall a squirrel's chase.
What wild adventures round they weave,
In harmony, we laugh and cleave.

The clouds above blend shades of fun,
As shadows in the daylight run.
With melodies that tickle each limb,
The symphony keeps spirits brimmed.

So let us sway, let voices chime,
With songs that dance through space and time.
In every note, a chuckle found,
In nature's laughter, we are bound.

Stanzas Shimmering on the Forest Floor

On forest floors, where light takes flight,
The mushrooms host an open mic night.
The critters gather for a show,
With puns as sweet as morning glow.

Amidst the ferns, the rabbits rhyme,
As hedgehogs beat the drums on time.
A tune so cheeky, they can't contain,
The giggles echo through the rain.

With every step, the leaves applaud,
As beetles give a little nod.
They sway and spin, a funky crew,
A chorus formed from nature's view.

So join the trail, where laughter reigns,
On forest floors, forget your pains.
With every stanza, every cheer,
We share the joy, embracing cheer.

Medleys of the Misted Moons

In the woods, a squirrel strums,
A tiny lute, while nature hums.
The raccoons join with pots and pans,
Creating sounds from woodland bands.

A rabbit hops, it plays the flute,
While fireflies dance, in cuter suits.
A chorus made of chirps and croaks,
The night bursts forth with laughing strokes.

Dances of Dreams and Dappled Light

A shadow twirls in leafy skirts,
While fairies gossip, waving their flirts.
The mushrooms cheer, they clap and shout,
As gnomes take turns to prance about.

With dappled rays on noses bright,
They jump around 'til out of sight.
The sunbeams giggle, they can't resist,
And join the dance, they feel a twist.

Division of the Dusk

At dusk, the owls hold court and jest,
With puns that put their wits to test.
A wise old crow brings in a pun,
That leaves the night with laughter spun.

They bicker over who has wings,
While crickets chime and softly sing.
A raccoon judge in a tiny hat,
Declares that all are great and fat.

Letters to the Leafy Knights

A letter penned to vines and thorns,
It tells of dreams when laughter warms.
The roots reply with sturdy rhymes,
While leaves declare they win all times.

The acorns chuckle, writing back,
With quips about a squirrel snack.
They roll in giggles on the ground,
As words of joy in jest abound.

Melodies Among the Trees

In the orchard, apples swing,
Singing tunes that make us grin.
Squirrels dance, they start to flail,
While the crows all hoot and wail.

Chirping frogs in offbeat time,
Dreaming up a funky rhyme.
Bees are buzzing with a beat,
Gathering nectar, quite the feat!

Down the path, a rabbit hops,
Leading all the woodland flops.
With a wiggle and a jig,
He joins in with a playful gig.

And when dusk draws close and swift,
The shadows seem to share a gift.
A playful breeze joins in the cheer,
While all the trees burst out in sneer.

Lullabies of the Woodland

Underneath the starlit glow,
A sleepy owl begins to show,
Hooting softly, offering dreams,
While raccoons weave their silly schemes.

The woodpecker taps in a fit,
As if searching for the right bit.
The badgers snore while hedgehogs spin,
Creating a ruckus with a cheeky grin.

Fireflies zigzag, oh what a sight,
Dancing around till the wings take flight.
Crickets chirp in a merry tune,
Guiding the night toward a new monsoon.

Frogs in chorus, croak out loud,
Filling the night, they draw a crowd.
Each lullaby's a funny jest,
Echoing nature's playful rest.

The Chorus of Twisting Vines

Twisting vines in a tangled race,
Brought together at a lively pace.
Bumblebees with a buzzing flair,
Join the vines, without a care.

Down below, the shadows prance,
Every twig gets caught in the dance.
Lizards laugh, with tails that shake,
Making up for every mistake.

Leaves are chuckling on the breeze,
Tickled by the whispering trees.
Every branch makes a quirky sound,
As laughter spreads o'er woodland ground.

And as the moon starts peeking through,
The vines hum songs of humor too.
Anechoic laughter fills the night,
With nature's joy, everything feels right.

Songs Beneath the Gnarled Branches

Gnarled branches with stories to share,
Invite critters without a care.
The worms wiggle in tune with the breeze,
While an old snail takes life with ease.

Underneath, the mushrooms sway,
Gladly joining the fun ballet.
A hedgehog trots with a haughty stance,
Challenging others to join the dance.

The wind brings whispers of delight,
Rustling leaves in a playful fight.
Raccoons giggle as they conspire,
While the ants march to their heart's desire.

With every sound, a tale unfolds,
In a world where laughter molds.
Beneath the gnarled branches so wild,
Nature sings, and joy runs mild.

Tales Carved in Bark

In the trees, the squirrels chatter,
Their acorns roll, a noisy patter.
The woodpecker's peck is quite a show,
While a rabbit hops to put on a glow.

The beaver wears a funny hat,
Imagining he's really quite flat.
The old owl hoots in a sarcastic tone,
As he watches the chaos from his throne.

A fox in boots struts on a log,
Claiming the title of the best dog.
With all this fuss, who needs a park?
These tales are born in the bark.

Verses in the Mist

In swirling fog, the rabbits dance,
With rhythm so odd, it's pure happenstance.
A turtle shuffles, slow but suave,
While birds tweet verses, a feathered rave.

The deer joke in a huddle of green,
Witty remarks about the unseen.
The shadows giggle; it's quite a sight,
As trees participate in the twilight.

A badger sings a silly tune,
As lightning bugs join for a swoon.
In misty groves where laughter lingers,
Nature's chaos plays on finger.

Crescendo of the Nightingale

A nightingale struts with flair and pride,
Singing loud like it's bonafide.
The crickets join in a brassy play,
While the moon grins its silver ray.

Mice tap dance, they're quite the teens,
In ill-fitting shoes from old cuisine.
A hedgehog slips, it's quite absurd,
As the audience roars, not a single word.

Saplings sway and twirl like pros,
In this grand show, anything goes.
Under stars with a twinkling glow,
Life's a laugh, and now you know!

A Tune for the Ancient Oaks

The oaks have stories gnarled and wise,
Yet they joke about their age and size.
Their leaves rustle, a chuckle shared,
With squirrels who think they're underprepared.

A raccoon's wearing a borrowed vest,
Claiming it's the ultimate quest.
The shadows cast a comical dance,
As all gather for the oak's grand prance.

A woodpecker joins with a clack and a tap,
As a fox sets the stage for a slapstick map.
The air is ripe with laughter and cheer,
In this leafy asylum, fun is near.

Poems of the Floating Ferns

Floating ferns on a quirky stream,
Carrying whispers of a rubber duck's dream.
They dance with laughter, twirl in delight,
While fish wear bowties, quite a sight!

Under their shade, the frogs start to croak,
Telling jokes that would make even rocks choke.
A snail gets tangled in a wild-haired vine,
Claiming it's trendy, feeling so fine!

The breeze brings giggles and soft little songs,
As squirrels gather, where each one belongs.
Mixing up nuts with the wildest cheer,
While tutus are spun, it's a fashion premiere!

So let the ferns float in all their splendor,
As nature's cabaret is a true contender.
With glee, they shimmer, a whimsical crew,
Making melody under the sky so blue!

A Silenced Songbird's Dream

A bird once chirped, but lost its song,
It puzzled the trees, where could it belong?
Instead, it pouted, folded its wings,
While tweeting in silence, it thought of lost flings.

Now in the night, it dreams quite absurd,
Of singing in tune while dressed as a nerd.
With glasses and bowties, a style so bold,
A comedy show in the branches unfolds!

It picks up a mic and struts on the stage,
Telling jokes of finches, it's all the rage!
The crickets start laughing, the owls roll their eyes,
As the breeze carries humor through starlit skies.

But its funniest act was a slip on a limb,
It flapped, lost its balance, oh how it did spin!
Yet all the forest erupted in cheer,
For songbirds in silence can still bring the jeer!

The Melancholy of the Dusk

The dusk tiptoes in with a sigh of the day,
It wears a gray cloak, feeling quite fey.
Stars are its friends, but they seem far away,
While shadows come out to dance and to play.

The moon strikes a pose, a dramatic affair,
As crickets start crooning, oh isn't it rare?
Alas, with a yawn, the sun bids goodbye,
While fireflies flicker like stars in the sky.

Yet twilight confesses it's not all despair,
For laughter in darkness blooms brightly with care.
A raccoon tells stories, as night slowly falls,
Of tricksters and mysteries, echoing calls.

So nightly they gather, a whimsical crew,
Celebrating dusk like a great silly brew.
In shadows they giggle, with stars up above,
For melancholy's at its funniest, love!

Harmonizing with the Hushed Tides

Waves whisper secrets to the sandy shore,
As shells start to giggle, oh what's in store?
The tides pull a prank, splashing with glee,
While the gulls squawk loudly, 'Join in the spree!'

The crabs form a band with a musical flair,
Dancing to rhythms of salt-laden air.
Starfish throw parties, they shine and they sway,
Inviting the jellyfish, bright in display.

But who steals the seashells? A mischievous fish,
With hopes of a treasure, oh what a wish!
Yet laughter erupts when it slips on a stone,
The ocean erupts in giggles alone.

So let the tides sing their playful refrain,
As the beach comes alive in this whimsical plane.
With humor and harmony, they share every tide,
Where the hushed waves of laughter can never hide!

Views from the Verdant Vault

Underneath the leafy arcs,
Squirrels scheme with crafty smirks.
They plot to steal my sandwich fast,
While birds just laugh and knit their quirks.

A mushroom once wore a tiny hat,
Claiming he's the king of snacks.
He whispered secrets to the ants,
While I just wondered where he's at.

The sun peeked in, a cheeky grin,
Tickling the leaves with bright delight.
The flowers danced, they took a spin,
While I just watched, with sheer delight.

A breeze brought tales of rubber ducks,
Floatin' in ponds with grinning frogs.
I giggled at their silly luck,
While sipping tea with the mossy logs.

The Trill of Time-touched Branches

A woodpecker played a loud beat,
On a branch that wobbled in tune.
He knocked and knocked, but missed the treat,
While I just chuckled at his boon.

The branches shook with gossip gay,
Old owls whispered tales of yore.
A hedgehog danced the night away,
While rabbits cheered and begged for more.

One squirrel tried to learn to fly,
Strapped feathers from a pillow fight.
He leaped from limb, oh my, oh my!
The branches quaked in sheer delight.

With acorns flying through the air,
Nutty chaos ruled the day.
Tree trunks shook without a care,
As laughter chased the clouds away.

The Heartbeat of Hemlock and Pine

In the forest where shadows hide,
A raccoon wore a crown of leaves.
He proclaimed himself as the guide,
While bees buzzed with their little thieves.

The conifers swayed, all in green,
Holding secrets of nature's song.
A tadpole crooned; he dreamed of wings,
While frogs croaked their approval strong.

Each twig held stories yet untold,
Of critters chasing dreams at night.
A lizard basked, so proud and bold,
While making faces at the light.

The air was thick with mischief's scent,
As fireflies danced without a care.
The rhythm of the woods, content,
Cradled joy in the evening air.

Hushed Romances in the Underbrush

Two ladybugs held hands one day,
In a garden lush and wide.
They whispered sweet things, come what may,
Amidst the leaves where love can hide.

A snail sought romance, slow and bright,
Wore a shell with sparkles like the sun.
He twirled around, quite the sight,
But missed his date, oh what a run!

Frogs croaked ballads, a serenade,
While hedgehogs listened, tails aglow.
The petals swayed, a lovely parade,
As romance bloomed, like flowers grow.

They tangled dreams beneath the moon,
In cozy nooks of mossy beds.
Where laughter played a happy tune,
And even thorns forgot their dreads.

Whispers in the Canopy

Squirrels in a fancy hat,
Planning for their acorn feast,
They dance and twirl and chat,
While avoiding the pesky east.

Birds gossip with flapping wings,
While frogs croak jokes that hit the leaf,
A raccoon joins with silly strings,
As laughter stirs beneath the reef.

The breeze tickles the branches high,
As shadows play a comical mime,
A caterpillar waves goodbye,
In a race against the winding time.

With each tumble and silly fall,
Laughter echoes through the wood,
Nature's choir begins to call,
In the funniest neighborhood.

Melodies of the Verdant Grove

A rabbit sings with a carrot mic,
To boisterous cheers from a gilded toad,
The fox struts in, thinking he's hype,
But slips on the spade, oh, what a load!

A bear taps feet on an old tree trunk,
While a mouse plays a tune on a thimble.
When the crowd erupts, there's no need for junk,
As all the forest critters simply tremble.

Giggling leaves join the jazzy beat,
The ants form a line, a parade so grand,
Each creature dances with two left feet,
Under the twinkling stars, hand in hand.

With every strum of the leafy harp,
They sway and spin, it's quite the sight,
A symphony of chuckles, a whimsical lark,
In a grove where the sun kisses the night.

Lullabies Among the Leaves

A sleepy snail hums a soft tune,
While a chatty parrot adds a cheer,
Fireflies flicker, glowing like moons,
In a night where dreams draw near.

Crickets chirp in a sleepy refrain,
With a turtle wearing a straw hat,
They lie by a pond, avoiding the rain,
And giggle at dreams they've had—imagine that!

Seeds toss whispers from tree to tree,
A raccoon sings tales of the day,
While a breeze joins in, ever so free,
As it carries the worries away.

So drift along in this leafy bed,
As lullabies dance through the night,
With whispers of laughter, where dreams are fed,
And all the world feels just right.

Echoes Under the Arbor

Beneath the arch of ivy's embrace,
A woodpecker jokes with a nutty grin,
The chubby badger runs the race,
With a ticklish breeze stirring within.

The sunlight spills like liquid gold,
While spiders weave threads of quirky design,
They giggle as secrets are softly told,
Hoping their webs turn into a shrine.

Chirps and squeaks blend in a song,
As butterflies flutter to join the play,
The frog harmonizes, it's never wrong,
While critters gather, come what may.

Under the arbor where laughter roams,
They share their hopes and tales untold,
In this merry realm, it feels like home,
Where echoes of joy are worth their weight in gold.

Symphonies of the Dappled Sunlight

The squirrel plays the ukulele,
While birds drum on the bark,
The sunbeams start a conga line,
And shadows dance, oh what a lark!

The grass sings softly to the bees,
As daisies twirl, quite bright and bold,
The ants, they're forming bands, you see,
In rhythm with the stories told.

A chipmunk dons a tiny hat,
Declares himself the grove's new king,
He leads the creatures in a chat,
About the joy the sunlight brings.

So grab your friends, don't be shy,
Join nature's madcap jubilee,
Where laughter scatters from the sky,
In this dappled symphony so free!

Whirling Whispers of the Wind

The breeze composes cheeky tunes,
As leaves start swaying in delight,
They tell the clouds of silly loons,
Who juggle raindrops in their flight.

A dandelion spins with grace,
While doves conduct the sweet refrain,
Their feathers flit in quick embrace,
In this windy, whimsical domain.

The chatter of the honeyed bees,
Sounds like a joke told in the shade,
They buzz and laugh, oh what a tease,
In gusts where playful pranks are made.

So let your laughter fill the air,
As wind bestows its gentle cheer,
In nature's theatre, none compare,
To whispers that you'll long hold dear!

The Dance of the Dappled Rays

Sunlight twirls with playful flair,
Through branches swaying to the beat,
They flicker like a bright affair,
On forest floors they bring the heat.

The fungi wear their party hats,
While shadows shimmy 'round the trees,
A raccoon juggles shiny spat,
With giggles from the buzzing bees.

The beetles join in on the fun,
With tiny tap shoes on their feet,
While laughter sparkles in the sun,
As critters gather for a treat.

They dance in circles, cut a rug,
Amidst the scent of blooming sage,
In this merry woodland slug,
Where sunlight writes an epic page!

Chants of the Enchanted Grove

In rhymes where squirrels quirk their tails,
And owls sing with a raspy glee,
The forest echoes with the tales,
Of woodland friends, so wild and free.

The toads croak out a funny verse,
While rabbits bounce along the floor,
In harmony, they all disperse,
To find new joys they can explore.

The shadows giggle softly loud,
As sunlight plays a game of peek,
The trees stand tall, a leafy crowd,
Cheering on this hilarious sneak.

So step into this merry fray,
Where laughter flows like bubbling brook,
In nature's witty, charming play,
Find magic in the pages' nook!

Serenades of the Swaying Branches

The squirrels dance like tiny clowns,
In search of acorns, dodging frowns.
With tails that whip and twirl around,
Their antics echo, joy unbound.

A crow caws loud, with quite a flair,
It struts with pride, without a care.
While shadows play, and giggles rise,
The trees conspire with whispered lies.

A breeze joins in, a gentle tease,
It rustles leaves, and they all freeze.
"What was that?" they blink with glee,
In this grand show of woodland spree.

So tune your heart to nature's jest,
Where laughter lives and never rests.
The branches sway, the ground will hum,
In serenades where joy is from!

Harmonics in the Woodland Shade

In a glen where shadows play,
A rabbit's party kicks off the day.
With carrots stacked like disco lights,
They bounce and hop in pure delight.

The raccoons sport their masks of gray,
And shimmy close to join the fray.
They flick their paws with rhythmic grace,
Making friends in this wild space.

An owl on high, with wisdom's guise,
Checks their moves with winking eyes.
"Keep it down," it hoots with cheer,
"Or risk the nap I hold so dear."

Yet all the fuss and merry sound,
Makes every creature dance around.
In woodland shade, where laughter blooms,
The harmonies dispel all glooms!

Rhythms of the Wandering Woods

With each step through leafy trails,
A gentle beat, no need for sails.
The brook babbles with tales to share,
While butterflies perform mid-air.

A fox, so sly, spins tricks galore,
Inviting friends to join the lore.
"Oh come on, friends, the fun's begun,
Let's turn the woods into our run!"

And now the beetles march in sync,
Conducted by a cricket's wink.
They prance and dance, all deemed elite,
In this woodland flash mob on their feet.

Through twists and turns, the forest laughs,
An open stage for nature's staff.
In rhythms found on dirt and leaves,
The plot thickens, everyone believes!

Odes to the Roots and Sky

Beneath the roots where secrets lie,
The gopher plots, oh my, oh my!
With tiny shovels, dreams laid low,
He schemes to snag a wormy show.

The birds above, they croon and sing,
While squirrels round the branches swing.
"Catch that tune, oh great blue jay,
Break out your best, don't fade away!"

A beaver chews on branches near,
His woodwork skills are quite a cheer.
With sticks and dreams, he builds a dam,
Crowning all with nature's glam.

So raise your cups to roots so deep,
And skies where mischief starts to leap.
For in this realm of giggles spry,
We toast the wild, oh my, oh my!

Echoing Harmonies of the Ancient Trees

In the branches, squirrels prance,
While owls keep watch with a curious glance.
Their hoots loop laughter in the air,
Nature's jokes, everywhere!

The wind plays tunes on leafy sprites,
Dancing shadows in playful heights.
A chipmunk choruses in perfect rhyme,
As if it knows the timing's prime!

Bark-studded grandmas tell silly tales,
Of past adventures and woodland fails.
With every rustle, laughter rolls,
In the heart of the forest, where humor strolls.

The trees chuckle as breezes tease,
Pinecones drop like musical keys.
While critters join in, they all agree,
Life's a jest in this nature spree!

Reverberations of the Woodland Spirits

Mischief abounds in the underbrush,
Where leaf sprites giggle, in a rush.
Their voices echo, a spirited cheer,
With every giggle, the trees bend near.

Beneath the moon's watchful grinning glow,
A raccoon juggles acorns in a row.
With each slip, a chorus of 'oops' rings,
The woodland chorus, hilariously sings!

A fox in a top hat tips with delight,
Dancing shadows in the soft moonlight.
While rabbits break into a fun ballet,
Chasing fireflies that flit away!

The spirits grin with their twinkling eyes,
As nature's jesters bring grand surprise.
In the heart of the woods, they find their stake,
Crafting giggles in every quake!

Aria of the Wandering Stream

Bubbling brooks with a playful glee,
Tickle the rocks, dance merrily.
With every splash, a chuckle escapes,
As frogs in tuxedos join the shapes!

The pebbles giggle, they adore the chat,
From water's whispers to a wise old bat.
"Why did the river cry?" the shadows tease,
"Because it's too deep for any sneeze!"

As fish flip-flop in synchronized lines,
They laugh at the ducks in their wobbly designs.
The current hums a silly tune,
Under the watchful eye of the moon.

Drifting leaves join the watery tune,
Spirits of laughter beneath the raccoon.
Every ripple holds a giggle's glow,
In the aria of the stream's delightful flow!

Sonatas of the Sunlit Glades

In the meadow, beams of gold,
Spin tales that never get old.
Daisies twirl in a clumsy dance,
Each petal seems to take a chance!

The butterflies host a comic play,
With silly antics throughout the day.
A drunk bumblebee zig-zags by,
He laughs so hard, he forgets to fly!

The sunlight cracks jokes through gaps of trees,
While grasshoppers giggle with such ease.
They chirp along to the sonorous cheer,
"Hop a little higher, we have no fear!"

In glades where sunlight winks and gleams,
Laughter ripples through the dreams.
With every rustle, joy seems to grow,
In this symphony, where giggles flow!

Ballads Under the Canopy

In the wood where squirrels tease,
I sang a tune as loud as bees.
A raccoon danced, oh what a sight,
Claiming my sandwich, what a bite!

The owls rolled eyes, they're such a hoot,
While critters gathered underfoot.
A rabbit joined with jazzed-up flair,
Even the trees swayed without care!

The winds whispered secrets of the day,
As chipmunks stole the show, hooray!
Laughter echoed through the leaves,
In this place where joy achieves.

So come on down, let laughter flow,
Where tunes are played, and no one's slow.
The canopy holds more than shade,
It's where the best memories are made!

Cadence in the Clearing

In the glade where mischief brews,
I lost my shoe, oh what a muse!
A fox in specs wrote up a play,
With no respect for word display!

The chorus chirped, the crickets laughed,
While butterflies shared a wild draft.
My pants got stuck on thorny vines,
As frogs chimed in with grand designs!

The trees applauded with their leaves,
While I was tangled in my sleeves.
A dance-off started with a pout,
And soon I joined, no doubt about!

So here we gather, light and free,
With silly antics under the tree.
In this clearing where giggles reign,
We'll turn missteps into our gain!

The Story Within the Roots

Down low where whispers softly crawl,
A tale unfolds, just for us all.
With gnarled roots that twist and twine,
They gossip of a silly dine!

The mice host parties, cheese galore,
While ants perform their vaudeville chore.
A snail with flair stole the limelight,
In a slow-motion dance, what a sight!

The shadows chuckled, secrets they keep,
As the old trees sang the songs of sheep.
With every step, a new riddle played,
I nearly fell, my balance swayed!

So listen close to the roots that bind,
For laughter's hidden in every kind.
Among the quirks and tales so deep,
Are funny stories that make you leap!

Sonnet of the Silhouetted Shadows

In twilit realms where shadows prance,
The night is young; they love to dance.
A cat in shades pulls off a twist,
While shadows play in latest mist!

A ghostly figure strums a tune,
Under the glow of a hazy moon.
The hedgehogs join, their style is rare,
Throwing their quills in the evening air!

The owls approve with a wink and nod,
As shadows spin, it seems quite odd.
The moonlight's laughter fills the night,
Encouraging shadows in their flight!

So join the fest where giggles grow,
In silhouettes, let your joy flow.
With shadows dancing, don't stand still,
For in this night, we always will!

The Lament of Leaves Lost

Once I was a leaf so green,
Swaying in the breeze, you see,
But now I'm stuck on Fido's tail,
A prankster's move, oh what a fail!

My friends all dance in autumn air,
While I just cling, it's quite unfair.
They twirl and flutter, it's pure delight,
I envy them with all my might.

They laugh at me, the silly fool,
As I become a pet's new tool.
The birds do chirp their merry song,
I'll join them, but I've been here too long!

So here's to leaves, both bold and brave,
And all the tales that nature gave.
But spare a thought for lonely me,
Stuck on a dog—my fate's so funny!

Verses Woven with Shadows

In the shade where shadows play,
A gnome once danced in bright ballet.
His moves were silly, quite a sight,
He tripped on roots and took to flight!

A squirrel laughed, perched on a ledge,
"He's better off by yonder hedge!"
But gnomes are hard and never quit,
He landed safe on a tree split.

The flowers giggled in their bloom,
As antics filled the forest gloom.
A melody of rustling leaves,
A symphony of playful thieves.

These verses rise with shadows' sway,
In nature's song, we join the play.
Each twist and turn, a joyous feat,
Echoes of laughter, oh so sweet!

The Ballad of Bark and Breeze

Once there was a tree named Fred,
Who spoke to breezes as he said:
"I'll tell you jokes, oh so divine,
But mind the birds; they steal the line!"

The wind just chuckled, twirling leaves,
While Fred recounted all his thieves.
"Those pesky critters hear me brag,
And send their singers in my rag!"

But bark was tough; he jeweled with glee,
"I'll ruffle feathers, wait and see!"
With each gust, he shared a jest,
Creating chaos, all in jest.

So here's to trees in winds that flow,
As bark and breeze put on a show.
Each laugh rings out from branch to ground,
In nature's theater, joy is found!

Fantasies in Fragrant Foliage

In fragrant groves where dreams take flight,
    A fairy hops from leaf to light.
She rides on scents of blooming cheer,
    Tickling petals with her sneer.

"Why do you frown, oh flower bright?
I'll paint your day with sheer delight!"
But daisies sighed and petals drooped,
    As fairies giggled, slyly stooped.

"Come, join the dance!" they called with glee,
    But violets just wished for tea.
"Let's bake a cake or share a laugh,
    Not twirl around in nature's path!"

So here they twinkle, blend, and croon,
    In silly tones beneath the moon.
A world of whimsy, oh what fun,
    Where fantasies and foliage run!

Notes in the Embrace of Nature

The squirrels dance with flair,
Chasing dreams through the air.
A bird drops a tune, oh so sweet,
As rabbits tap dance on fluffy feet.

A frog croaks a joke, quite absurd,
While bees hum along, undeterred.
The leaves shake with laughter, you see,
Nature's own comedy spree!

A worm winks with a cheeky grin,
Says, "I am the one who will win!"
The daisies giggle, all in a row,
With petals that flutter, putting on a show.

So join in this cheer, let's not be shy,
With nature's whimsy, we can fly high.
The forest is alive with a joyful song,
In this playful realm, we all belong.

Murmurs of the Enchanted Woodland

In the woodland, secrets are spun,
By the chatter of chipmunks having fun.
A snail races slow, what a sight,
While mushrooms giggle, oh what a delight!

The trees whisper tales of the day,
As the old owl hoots, "Come out and play!"
Bats hang upside down, making their bets,
On who will win the next silly sets.

The creek sings a tune, all a-flutter,
While frogs serenade with a ribbit and patter.
The flowers nod their heads in glee,
They've got the rhythm, can you feel the spree?

Laughs echo among branches high,
With twinkling stars winking in the sky.
The forest is humming, with joy we partake,
In this whimsical world, let's dance and shake!

Harmonies Beneath the Twilight Canopy

As sunset paints the sky with flair,
Crickets chirp tunes without a care.
A fox leads a conga line of sorts,
While fireflies join in, lighting courts.

The moon grins down with a silver glow,
Mice can't help but put on a show.
With acorn hats and leaves for capes,
They twirl and spin with silly shapes.

Raccoons juggle berries with great style,
While owls chuckle softly, keeping dial.
The twilight canopy drips with fun,
Nature's night is never done.

So pull up a leaf, and join the fun,
With laughter and music, together we run.
The night is young, so take a chance,
In this enchanted place, let's dance!

Ballads in the Heart of the Thicket

In the thicket, stories unfold,
With rabbits dressed in jackets of gold.
They sing of adventures under a tree,
While hedgehogs roll in glee, full of glee.

A wise old turtle begins to rap,
With beats that make every critter clap.
The shadows sway to every sound,
As laughter and joy spins all around.

The fawns prance about with grace and flair,
Jugglers of acorns, floating in air.
The fox strums a lute, quite out of tune,
Yet all join in, making melodies swoon.

In this thicket, where nonsense bloats,
And every creature finds laughter in notes.
Join the merry band, the music's enough,
With jest and cheer, let's fill the tough!

Whims of Wind and Nature

The squirrels conspire with cheeky delight,
They stash all the acorns and hide them from sight.
Crickets are crooning their tunes on a spree,
While bees dance around like they own all the trees.

The breeze sweeps through softly, a tickle, a tease,
It pulls at my hat and it makes my knees freeze.
Leafy confetti comes down with a shout,
As I trip on a root, with a flail and a pout.

A raccoon with swagger strolls in with style,
He pauses to wink and then flashes a smile.
The woodpecker's drumming, its beat full of cheer,
Makes me bop to the rhythm, forgetting my fear.

Nature's a circus, each day seems a show,
With laughter and antics, where silliness flows.
I giggle aloud at the chaos around,
In a world so alive, joy's never drowned!

Chronicles of the Canopied Realm

Upon branches high, where the chittering plays,
The monkeys are plotting their tricky arrays.
With cheeky bananas and toucans in tow,
It's a party up there, come join in the show!

The shadows grow larger, a dance step gone wrong,
As the owls hoot out lyrics to an offbeat song.
A fox wearing glasses is reading a book,
All the while giving the passersby a look.

In this leafy kingdom where giggles abound,
Every rustle and whisper is funny profound.
The ants form a conga and march with great pride,
While the butterflies flutter, bright colors collide.

From acorns to laughter, the stories they tell,
Of creatures and capers that don't end so well.
Each leaf holds a giggle, each breeze spins a tale,
In this realm of the canopied, joy shall prevail!

Echoes of the Evening Stars

When twilight descends and the fireflies flash,
The frogs croak a tune, their chorus a splash.
I spot a raccoon who's wearing a hat,
Dancing in circles – oh, imagine that!

The stars peek down, they wink and they giggle,
While crickets perform, causing hearts to wiggle.
A hedgehog rolls past, with a wink and a grin,
He's saving a seat – come and let's join in!

The moon's glowing bright, like a lamp in the night,
While shadows play games, trying to give fright.
"Who's there?" I call out, feeling a bit brave,
A raccoon responds: "Just your local knave!"

With laughter and echoes filling the breeze,
Nature's a party, put your cares at ease.
The world's quite the riddle, full of jests and jesters,
In the twilight's embrace, we become all investors!

Symphonies of Twilight

When twilight sings a goofy tune,
The crickets start their night brigade.
A squirrel dances to the moon,
In search of nuts, he's quite displayed.

A raccoon leaps, a splashy scene,
With berries stuck upon his nose.
He giggles with a cheeky glean,
And steals the show with his quick prose.

The fireflies wink like disco lights,
As owls hoot their jovial cheers.
No one can help but feel delight
While nature's laughter fills our ears.

So raise a glass to nature's fun,
Where twilight tales and tomfoolery blend.
Under the stars, we run and run,
In this frolic, joy won't end.

Odes to the Wind-Whipped Leaves

The leaves are shouting, 'Catch us quick!'
With gusts that tease and twirl about.
They swirl like dancers in a flick,
And scold the grass with a cheeky shout.

A squirrel's hat flies off in fright,
While acorns scatter like a game.
The branches sway with pure delight,
As if to claim the winds' own fame.

Oh, laughter echoes through the boughs,
With whispers soft, the trees respond.
A ticklish breeze on nature's brows,
As leaf and laugh are wittily conned.

So join the fun, don't miss the day,
In breezy winds, let giggles soar.
For nature plays, in its own way,
A silly song forevermore.

Choral Calls from the Canopy

In the canopy, a chorus sings,
Of birdy banter and monkey glee.
A toucan shares his brightest wings,
While parrots jest, "You can't catch me!"

A sloth interjects from his high perch,
With jokes that make the branches shake.
His humor's slow, but packed with search,
For every laugh is worth the wait!

The sunbeams peek through every leaf,
In laughter's glow, we're all entwined.
From treetop tales of joy and grief,
To chorus lines, hilariously lined.

So heed the call, join in the fun,
In nature's choir, all voices play.
For through the branches, laughter's spun,
In joyful harmony, we sway.

Aria of Arbor and Sky

An aria floats through branches wide,
As a kitten chases a shadowed spark.
With every leap, she takes such pride,
    As birds gossip in their lofty arc.

An old dog naps under the sun,
    Awakens for a quick panache.
He dreams of steaks, his idea of fun,
While bees buzz by in a sunny thrash.

Oh, playful winds, with laughter rife,
Tickle the leaves, and stir the blights.
With joy and jest, we share our life,
In nature's humor found in heights.

So sing along, join nature's play,
With giggles caught in every sigh.
For here we find in nature's sway,
    An aria bright that will not die.

Echoes in the Shade

In the shade where shadows play,
A squirrel sings, then skips away.
The owls chuckle, loud and clear,
While rabbits dance, let's not get near.

A breeze confesses secrets old,
While leaves gossip, tales retold.
The chipmunks laugh, their humor bright,
As crickets chirp through day and night.

The frogs recite a silly rhyme,
With lyrics lost in space and time.
Their voices echo, soft and keen,
A woodland choir, quite the scene!

Under boughs, where giggles weave,
The laughter spins, it won't deceive.
A funny world, so wild and free,
Join in the jest, come sing with me!

Rhythms of the Forest Floor

The forest floor, a dance so bright,
With mushrooms twirling, what a sight!
A beetle trips, he takes a spill,
While shadows chuckle, what a thrill!

Ants marching in a line so neat,
With tiny hats, they tap their feet.
A snail slides in, all slow and glum,
But then he joins, and boom! He's fun!

The laughter rolls like pebble streams,
In the leaves, where sunlight beams.
Each rustle plays a playful note,
As melodies weave from root to throat.

Watch the forest, a jest unfolds,
With every giggle, life enfolds.
A funny rhythm, soft and pure,
Come dance along, let's all be sure!

Serenade of the Swaying Leaves

Leaves are swaying, what a sight,
Whispering jokes in morning light.
They tease the breeze, a playful game,
While branches giggle, quite the fame!

The sun peeks through, a funny chap,
Catching shadows, in a nap.
A raccoon juggles acorns bright,
As butterflies take in the light.

The trees all sway in harmony,
As squirrels plot a heist of glee.
A wren hops in, her song so true,
She sings the laugh, just for you!

Underneath this leafy dome,
Nature sways, it feels like home.
Let's join the fun, the songs, the tease,
With nature's cheer, we laugh with ease!

The Strum of Nature's Heart

Nature strums a quirky tune,
While raccoons dance beneath the moon.
The fireflies blink in symphony,
A show of lights, it's wild and free!

The river hums its playful song,
As frogs leap in, they can't go wrong.
A bear joins in with gentle grace,
A clumsy waltz, a furry face!

The wind picks up, a fiddle plays,
It dances through the leafy maze.
The stars all wink, a twinkling jest,
As laughter echoes, we're all blessed!

So come, my friend, let's strum along,
In nature's arms where we belong.
With every beat, in joy we part,
Together, we'll feel nature's heart!

Enchantment on the Outer Boughs

A squirrel juggles acorns with flair,
While birds debate tunes, caught up in the air.
The branches chuckle, as leaves start to sway,
In a dance of mishaps, they laugh all the way.

A raccoon wears spectacles, reading a map,
While turtles enjoy a leisurely nap.
The whispers of nature, a comical scene,
As the breeze rolls by, tickling leaves so green.

Frogs leap in chorus, croaking a laugh,
While bugs form a band on a tree's sturdy staff.
The sun winks down with a playful glow,
As shadows join in for an impromptu show.

The owls hoot nonsense, wise in their way,
While bees do the cha-cha, busy as they play.
An enchantment unfolds, amidst giggles and cheer,
Nature's grand circus, let's all gather here!

Refrain of the Rolling Hills

On rolling hills, where the daisies do prance,
A rabbit in sneakers takes off in a dance.
The butterflies giggle, swirling around,
As the grass tries to dance, but falls to the ground.

The flowers hold debates on who smells the best,
While ants in a line form their own little fest.
Each pebble a comedian, cracking a joke,
As clouds overhead giggle, slowly they poke.

The wind carries whispers of laughter and joy,
A child with a kite plays like a toy.
While squirrels throw pinecones, an acorn brigade,
With each silly mishap, the hills serenade.

The hills will remember, the fun that they had,
With giggles and tumbles, oh, wasn't it rad?
A refrain of laughter echoing high,
As the sun sets softly, painting the sky!

Tropes in the Treetops

In tall treetops, where the antics reside,
Monkeys tell tales, with humor as their guide.
A parrot critiques, with a wink and a squawk,
While squirrels reenact old stories to mock.

The branches, they giggle, in a rustle of leaves,
As critters exchange their most clever of thieves.
A fox in a top hat bows with a flair,
As the owls look on, with their knowing stare.

Each evening a puppet show, just for the crew,
Raccoons put on masks, and the skunks join in too.
The dusk brings a hush, yet laughter still swells,
Among all the tropes that the tall treetops tell.

For every mishap, there's laughter to share,
Nature's own comedy unfolding midair.
With jokes and with giggles, the treetops unite,
In a nightly performance, under soft starlight!

Fragmented Whispers of Time

In the forest of moments, where echoes collide,
A bee spills the tea on what squirrels confide.
The clock knows it's late, but the owls can't agree,
While the frogs round the pond laugh in glee.

Each shadow a tale, each flickering light,
Fungi hold secrets, wild and bright.
The crickets do stand-up, with rhythm divine,
As the stars wink above, a cosmic design.

The past and the present twist into laughs,
A turtle with sass takes quick little baths.
Each fragment of time holds a moment of fun,
As the moon rolls her eyes, the night's just begun.

The whispers keep flowing, so vivid, so clear,
In the woods, oh the stories, let's lend them an ear.
With each hearty chuckle, a riddle shall chime,
In the fragile embrace of fragmented time.

The Echo of Forgotten Stories

In a park where trees do whisper,
The squirrels hold a secret twister.
They chat of nuts and acorn deeds,
While slipping past our human needs.

Old tales of branches take a flight,
As birds raise songs to morning light.
Yet we just chuckle, they don't see,
Their epic tales of lunch and spree.

A wise old owl joins in the game,
Claims he's the one who found fame.
But all he's got is fluff and surprise,
His stories float like leaves in the skies.

So let's sit back and hear the cheer,
As ancient tales tickle our ear.
For every whisper on the breeze,
There's a hint of laughter in the trees.

Rhyme of the Rustling Grass

In fields where blades conspiring sway,
The grass sings songs of yesterday.
A chorus formed of bugs and breeze,
Composing tunes with such great ease.

A cricket jumps, his notes so bold,
He thinks he's grand, just like of old.
While ants parade with tiny drums,
Creating beats as laughter comes.

But oh, the wind, it steals the show,
With giggles swirling to and fro.
Each rustle spins a new charade,
In grassy symphonies we've made.

So dance along, don't be too shy,
Join in the fun, let spirits fly.
For in this grassy, silly pass,
We find the joy that fills our glass.

Sagas in the Daily Light

Each morning brings a tale untold,
Of mischief that the sun unfolds.
A cat with dreams of being grand,
Plots each pounce with clever hand.

The dog, though loyal, thinks it's neat,
To chase his tail on sunny street.
While pigeons gossip overhead,
Of crumbs and chaos, lightly spread.

Neighbors laugh with coffee in hand,
As squirrels perform their nutty band.
These daily scripts, a chuckle feast,
With jests that never seem to cease.

So raise your mug and toast the day,
To silly scenes that come our way.
For laughter rings with every blink,
In life's grand play, we chuckle and think.

Lyrical Shadows and Shimmering Leaves

In gardens lush with shimmering hues,
The shadows dance in playful views.
Leaves that giggle as they fall,
Stir up laughter, a merry call.

Each rustling page, a fleeting tale,
Of flowered dreams and silly trails.
A bee, though busy, hums in tune,
To sunny days and balmy noon.

The sunbeams wink, a prancing face,
As petals twirl in a lovely race.
While frogs recite their little quirks,
Each croak a spark, as nature smirks.

So join this jest of leaf and breeze,
Find joy in whispers among the trees.
For in each shadow, laughter thrives,
In lyrical worlds where whimsy dives.

Folklores of the Flora

In a garden where daisies dance,
A gopher wore a bright-eyed glance.
He told tales of why worms can sing,
While wearing a hat made of spring.

The tulips giggled, the roses blushed,
As a snail on the path was hushed.
They whispered of bees who plot and play,
And how bugs always nap on sunny days.

A daffodil swayed with great delight,
Claiming it could outshine the moonlight.
While violets shared secrets so old,
Of the radish who dreamed of being bold.

So wander and listen, oh curious friend,
The tales of the sprigs that never end.
For in every bloom, a riddle is spun,
Of laughter and friendships under the sun.

The Singing Earth

Beneath a tree that croons at dawn,
A squirrel practices with a yawn.
He plays the nuts like a raucous band,
With acorns clapping, it's quite unplanned.

The soil hums a goofy tune,
While daisies sway and chase the moon.
The worms join in, with wiggly cheer,
A soil symphony, oh far and near!

The grasshoppers leap, the beetles brawl,
A classic bickering, echoing all.
With tunes so catchy, you'll spin and twirl,
Defining a dance in a leafy swirl.

Each note is a giggle, a chuckle, a fit,
As flowers take center stage and commit.
So sing along, let your voice soar high,
In this melody made under the sky.

Patterns of the Playful Wind

The wind blew through the whispering pines,
Tickling the leaves with cheeky designs.
A butterfly rode on its silly back,
On a journey mapped by a giggling quack.

Clouds drifted lazily, full of jest,
Crafting shadows where toads like to rest.
With a wink and a bounce, they hop and cheer,
Serenading the daisies, spreading their cheer.

A kite got tangled in a tree's embrace,
Demanding a squirrel's mischievous grace.
"Untangle me quick!" the kite did implore,
"Or I'll become a bird's latest lore!"

So spinning and darting, each breeze a delight,
The wind tosses laughter to last through the night.
With playful adventures that twirl and ping,
Life's dizzying dance, oh what joy it brings!

Vibrations from the Veiled Glade

In a glade where shadows intertwine,
A raccoon is practicing his best moonshine.
With a banjo made from a hollowed-out stump,
He strums and forgets about every bump.

The toadstools joined in, with hats askew,
Imitating humans, quite a funny view.
As fireflies twinkled in rhythm divine,
They danced to the tune of the nighttime line.

A hedgehog with glasses, wise and astute,
Says, "Life's a joke, so stay resolute!"
With each quirky note, a chuckle erupts,
As pixies descend and do little jumps.

So wander through laughter, let giggles flow,
In this hidden glade where the wild things grow.
For here in this haven of whimsy and cheer,
The heart learns to lighten, with joy ever near.

Songs of the Rustling Foliage

The leaves have secrets, they wiggle and sway,
Whispering gossip about the squirrel's play.
A raccoon in a mask, talks big about cheese,
While birds mock his antics, as they laugh in the trees.

A bunny hops by, on his way to the show,
Practicing dance moves, with a wild, springy flow.
The blue jays clap wings, in rhythm and cheer,
Nature's own band, oh, what a delight here!

A woodpecker knocks like a drummer so bold,
But he's really just bored, that's a story retold.
The owls roll their eyes, in wise old repose,
While critters all joke, in their leafy clothes.

So gather round, friends, hear this jolly tune,
In this lively place, where all dance and swoon.
With laughter and joy, we embrace nature's song,
In this whimsical world where we all belong.

Tales from the Timbered Realm

In the realm where the tall trees argue and bicker,
A fox tells a tale, it's a real knee-slapper.
He claims he once strutted in a three-piece suit,
But tripped on a root, and fell on his snoot!

A deer rolls her eyes, and says with a grin,
'This place is a hoot, let the fun times begin!'
A turtle with glasses recites limericks grand,
'Of running so fast, but I still need to stand!'

The owls hoot with laughter, their wisdom on hold,
'The stories here never get tired or old.'
Squirrels join in, throwing acorns to cheer,
Each nut encapsulating a giggle or sneer.

So gather the critters, let's spread the delight,
With tales of mishaps, that last through the night.
In the timbered realm, oh what fun we will weave,
For laughter and joy, is what we believe!

Chants of the Winding Trails

Down the twisting path, where the shenanigans grow,
A rabbit sings loud, 'It's a talent show!'
With a coat made of fluff, her act is quite grand,
But she loses her script, leaves it all unplanned!

A raccoon with rhythm beats on a stump,
While squirrels do backflips, in a feathery lump.
The birds yell, 'Encore!' in a flurry of song,
But the raccoon gets tangled, and it all goes wrong!

The laughter erupts, on the windy trail bends,
Even shy little hedgehogs find courage as friends.
The trees sway along, like they're part of the play,
In this woodland waltz, come join the hooray!

So take a stroll here, where the fun never fails,
Join each merry creature, on these winding trails.
In a world full of giggles, let your spirit be free,
For the joy of the woods sings, in harmony!

Verses Cradled by the Forest

In the forest so lush, with a sparkle and twinkle,
A hedgehog in glasses begins to sprinkle,
His jokes in the air, like confetti of fun,
While mushrooms chime in, 'Hey, look at us run!'

The trees sway in rhythm, grooving all day,
As squirrels play jazz, in their nutty ballet.
The owls take the stage, with wisecracks to throw,
While the deer play the tambourine, all aglow!

A beaver brings snacks, in his clever disguise,
With fruit from the woods, oh, what a surprise!
'Let's snack and recite,' is his cheerful decree,
As the night drapes in laughter, under stars like confetti.

So gather your friends, for the night is now set,
With verses and giggles, there's no time for regret.
In the cradle of nature, where joy's on a spree,
Each verse and each tale, is a party for free!

Sonnet of Shadows and Light

In the dance of shadows, a squirrel took flight,
Chasing sunbeams that sparkled so bright.
A crow cawed with laughter, perched high on a gate,
While the dog in the yard plotted all kinds of fate.

Down by the bushes, a lizard slipped by,
Wearing sunglasses because he was shy.
He winked at a bird who sang out a tune,
Mixing jazz with a hoot under the moon.

A chipmunk juggled acorns with flair,
But tripped on a root, sent them flying in air.
The forest erupted in raucous applause,
As nature united in laughter because.

So let's raise a toast with a cup of dew,
To the chaos of critters, both old friends and new.
In the twilight, they frolic, they leap, and they play,
Under shadows and light, in the silliest way.

Nocturnal Chants of the Green Realm

Amidst the whispers of a moonlit grove,
A raccoon dined out—what a curious trove!
With a top hat and cane, he serenely partook,
Of leftovers left by an overnight cook.

The frogs held a concert, croaking the beat,
While fireflies flickered in their tiny retreat.
A raccoon in tuxedo swung to the sound,
As the owls rolled their eyes at the ruckus they found.

With grins on their faces, the crickets all chirped,
While the weary old fox just sat and then burped.
"Why fret about hush?" said a wise old toad,
"We've a midnight buffet on this glorious road!"

So here's to the nights when the weirdos unite,
In the depths of the forest, where laughter takes flight.
For amidst all the chaos, there's music to share,
In this green realm of giggles, we banish despair.

Whispers in the Canopy

In the treetops, the chatter can hardly be tamed,
As squirrels debate which branch should be claimed.
One holds a nut, wearing a crown made of leaves,
While the others just giggle, plotting their thieves.

A parrot critiques the attire of a deer,
"The stripes aren't quite right, you hear what I hear?"
The deer rolled his eyes, brushed off the remark,
While the parrot just squawked in the light of the dark.

A raccoon with style, in shades of cool grey,
Danced to the rhythm of leaves and of play.
The flowers shook petals—"Join in for a while!"
As the beetles would waltz, in a fanciful style.

Up high in the branches, the gossip takes flight,
While the creatures below just laugh at the sight.
In the canopy's heart, where the quirkiest thrive,
They share all their stories, keeping humor alive.

Harmonies of Leaf and Sky

A tune plucked from twigs danced on the breeze,
As toads threw a party beneath ancient trees.
With salsa and limbo, they wiggled with glee,
While the owls stood by, craving their tea.

Melodies woven with rustling leaves,
The mushrooms provided quite fancy reprieves.
A rabbit in bowtie served snacks with a hop,
While the wasps DJ'd—"You can't make me stop!"

The stars twinkled softly, providing the stage,
For a raccoon magician, who turned a new page.
He pulled out a carrot, to everyone's cheer,
As the crowd cried, "Encore! Bring on the beer!"

So gather 'round, friends, in this whimsical show,
Where nature's musicians put on quite a throw.
In the harmonies shared, let your laughter entwine,
In this symphony wild, we're all feeling fine.

Tales in the Treetops

In a tree a squirrel danced,
He tipped his hat and pranced.
A crow began to caw and fuss,
'Why not share your acorn thus?'

The owl hooted, quite bemused,
While the rabbit looked confused.
'These critters really know how to play,'
Said the raccoon, munching away.

The Burgeoning Verse

A poem sprouts with every rhyme,
Like mushrooms popping up in time.
A playful breeze begins to tease,
And brings the birds to dance with ease.

The squirrel writes on bark with glee,
While bees hum tunes from flower to tree.
A lilac blushes, then breaks the news,
'You won't find a verse that can't amuse!'

The Elusive Forest Echo

In the woods, what do you hear?
A giggle, then a whispered cheer.
A raccoon claims he's lost his hat,
The fox just laughs and says, 'What's that?'

An echo floats through leafy glades,
'Tell that to the chipmunk who parades!'
He struts around, quite full of pride,
While laughter ripples through the wide.

Narratives of the Night

Underneath the moonlit stage,
A toad croaks out the latest page.
The cricket chirps a tune quite slick,
'This nocturnal life, oh what a trick!'

A firefly shines, like popcorn popped,
The owl's wink says, 'Oh, I'm not stopped!'
Each tale spins in the dusky air,
Of acorn heists and shoes to wear.

www.ingramcontent.com/pod-product-compliance
Lightning Source LLC
Chambersburg PA
CBHW072146200426
43209CB00051B/753